BEFORE YOU RENT

All You Need To Know About Searching, Inspecting, Negotiating, And Moving In

Copyright 2010
KMS Publishing.com

Most consider renting more practical and sensible nowadays compared to the high-cost of owning real property. If you're not ready to buy your own house, renting is the next best thing to living independently and the closest thing to being the owner of your very own home.

Renting property is a big responsibility and there are actually real issues that you need to take into account prior to signing that contract that will bind you, and may turn out to constrain you, for several years. This book is your complete guide to renting your own house or apartment. You will learn all you need to consider prior to making the deal final.

- Understand your personal considerations for renting an apartment or house. What are you looking for? What are your needs versus your wants? What is your budget? Do you need a house or an apartment?

- Know important details on apartment and house hunting so your search is organized and productive.

- Learn the basic application requirements as a prospective tenant so you can put in order your personal and financial information all set for the background and credit check.

- Discover key details on negotiating, finalizing, and terminating your lease agreement.

- Find out if you really need the services of a professional real estate agent or agency.

Discover all you need to consider about renting before signing anything and moving in. You can get that apartment or house you desire without spending loads of money through the process of hunting, inspecting, negotiating and completing the deal!

TABLE OF CONTENTS

Introduction: The Benefits Of Renting _____ 8

1. Planning Based On Needs _____ 11

Size And Location Of Property _____ 11

Monthly Budget _____ 14

How Much Can You Afford? _____ 16

Sharing The Rent With A Roommate_____ 19

Extra Requirements _____ 22

Consider The Amenities _____ 23

Furnished Or Unfurnished? _____ 26
   Helpful Tips When Evaluating Furniture_____ 30
   Decorating A Rental House _____ 32
   Decorating A Rental Apartment _____ 34

Should You Rent A House Or An Apartment?
_____ 38

Rent To Own_____ 41

2. The Process Of Searching For Your New
Home_____ 44

Online Search _____ 46

Local Area Listings _____ 49

Helpful Search Tools And Queries _____ 51

Issues On Landlord_____ 52

3. Prospective Tenant Application _____ 56

Application Requirements For A Background
Check_____ 57

Personal Information _____ 58

Past And Present Status_____ 59

Character References _____ 60

A Credit Report Check _____ 62

Work On Your Credit Score _____ 63

Your Credit History _____ 65

Income And Employer Information_____ 66

Present An Actual Budget Blueprint That Explains Your
Ability To Pay _____ 69

4. Ocular Inspections _____ 70

What To Look For _____ 71

Compare Options _____ 80

5. Negotiating The Contract _____ 82

Your Rights And The Rights Of The Owner 83

Contract Terms To Scrutinize_____ 83

Deposit Requirements _____ 84

Payment Terms _____ 85

Rental Fees _____ 85

Termination Information _____ 86

Moving Stipulations _____ 87

Breaking The Contract _____ 87

Matters To Consider Prior To Breaking The Contract_ 88

Getting Your Security Deposit Back_____ 91

Read The Fine Print _____ 93

Read Your Contract Carefully _____ 94

Do You Need An Attorney? _____ 96

Key Tip: Everything In Writing _____ 97

Bargaining Tips_____ 98

Property Inspections_____ 99

6. Rental Agency Services_____ 101

What To Take Into Account _____ 101

Conclusion _____ 103

INTRODUCTION:
THE BENEFITS OF RENTING

While there are some renters who view renting an apartment or a house as a failure, there are others who see the benefits there are to be gained from renting a property as opposed to purchasing a property. Some of the benefits of renting include the ability to save money while renting for the purpose of purchasing a home, few maintenance requirements and the inclusion of amenities which the renter would not likely be able to afford if they were to purchase a home instead of renting. Although there are some negative aspects to renting an apartment, this article will focus exclusively on the benefits of renting a property.

The Ability to Save Money

Being able to save up a great deal of money for the purpose of making a down payment on a dream home is just one of the many great advantages to renting a property. Many homeowners were able to realize their dream of homeownership only after living in a rental property for a certain amount of time. Although renting is often criticized as throwing money away because it does not result in equity, the ability to save money while renting is unparalleled

Rent for an apartment is usually considerably less expensive than the monthly mortgage on a home. The home is also typically much bigger than the rental property but in cases where the renter is renting for the sole purpose of saving money, the value of renting cannot be denied. Depending on how long the renter stays in the apartment, they may save hundreds or even thousands of dollars during the course of the rental agreement.

No Maintenance Properties

Another advantage to renting a property is there is typically little or no maintenance required by the renter. This is especially true in an apartment situation. The renter may be responsible for small items such as changing light bulbs but more extensive repairs such as leaks in plumbing or clogs in drains are typically handled by the maintenance staff of the rental property.

Additionally common areas such as grassy areas or gardens are maintained by the maintenance staff. The exception is usually when the renter rents a home as opposed to the apartment. In these cases the renter may still not be responsible for small repairs but might be obligated to take care of items such as maintaining the grass.

Worthwhile Amenities

Another advantage to apartment living is often the amenities offered to residence. Such amenities might include usage of the pool, an exercise room, meeting spaces and a theater room. In most cases these amenities are offered free of charge to resident and their guests. Many renters who might be able to purchase a home would not likely be able to purchase a home with amenities such as a pool, fully equipped exercise room and a home theater.

These items are often considered luxurious and are not available in the majority of homes which are on the market at any particular time. In fact searching for homes which specifically have these features may severely limit the number of search results and may result in no search results at all when these features are searched in conjunction with a typical price range. However, those who rent can enjoy access to these amenities. They may pay more in rent than those in a comparable apartment complex without these amenities but they are also still likely saving a considerable amount of money each month as long as they are budgeting wisely and have chosen a rental property within their price range.

1.
PLANNING BASED ON NEEDS

As you set out into the world, looking for a new place to live, you will be tempted to just start viewing properties. You may find yourself looking at properties that have beautiful features located in just the right area. The problem is that the properties you may be looking at are unlikely to have the features that you need.

There is a big difference between needing and wanting when it comes to shopping for apartments or homes to rent. Before you dive into the market to check out what is available, take the time to process what you need first. This book will provide you with a look at what it takes to rent an apartment, condo or home from start to finish. Do not skip the all-important step of knowing what you need versus what you want.

Size And Location Of Property

The first two things to take into consideration when selecting an apartment or a house to rent, is the size of it and the location. Ask yourself the following questions:

- How many bedrooms do you need?
- Is it important to have an extra room for guests?
- Do you want an eat in kitchen or a dining room?
- How many bathrooms should the home have?
- Is there a need for a property that has an area for children to play?
- Do you need an area for pets?
- What other size requirements do you have?
- What about parking needs, does the property offer enough, secure parking for your needs?

It is important to distinguish between needs and wants here. Specifically, to need to ensure the property is big enough for your particular needs but not so big that it blows your budget out of the water. In most areas, size is directly related to cost.

The location of the property is also important. Most people realize that they would like to live in a specific area. Others are hoping to find a location that fits their needs.

If you are unfamiliar with an area, before renting a property there, ask your agent (if you are using one) to drive around the location. You can learn information about the city's safety levels, accommodations, and even which businesses are located within it by simply looking at the city's Chamber of Commerce website. If they do not have one, stop by the office to ask questions, pick up a map and to learn more.

Even if you are familiar with the area, there are a few things to keep in mind about it before you rent.

1. Does the location allow a quick commute to and from work? If not, factor this into higher gas costs as well as more time spent driving back and forth.
2. Does the location have easy to access to highways or freeways?
3. Does the area offer the shops, grocery stores and restaurants you need to have close enough to you?
4. More so, are you located so close to the busiest area of the city that you have to deal with loud noise and traffic?
5. Is the location in an area that you like? Being happy where you are living is an important aspect of finding the right place to live.

Location and property size is important. As you can tell, there are details in both areas that could be called desires rather than needs. Finding a balance is important. The key is to know your budget before shopping.

Monthly Budget

How much money do you have to spend every month on your rented house or apartment? This is more than just selecting a property that you like. It is also to look for one that you can afford. But, how much can you afford?

Before you even start looking at properties too closely, it is important to look at the numbers. Consider your current income and expenses to determine what amount of money you can put into an apartment.

Take a look at the following questions. Tally up the costs you are likely to have in your apartment or house. This can help you to determine the amount of money you can spend on the property you end up renting.

1. Tally up your income. List all sources of income that will be put towards paying any expenses related to the property.

2. Determine your non-housing related expenses. This includes paying credit card bills, personal loans, and car loans. Any expenses you are currently paying that will carry over should be included here.

3. Consider common utility costs. If you are unsure of any of these costs, speak with someone who is renting a similar sized

property in your area or you can later ask
the landlord about the estimated costs of
these.

    a. Electric costs
    b. Gas costs
    c. Cable and Internet, if you play to get
    d. Phone service
    e. Service costs such as refuse and
       sewers
    f. Other utility costs
    g. Taxes associated with the property,
       if any

4. Determine costs that are not constant each
   month. To get an estimate here, be sure you
   consider your current spending and the
   goals you may have.

    a. Food costs
    b. Fuel costs for vehicles
    c. Entertainment money
    d. Funds you are putting into savings
    e. Money used for clothing or other
       purchases

5. Factor in costs associated with setting up
   the property such as the cost of furniture
   and appliances you may need.

Now that you have these details, subtract all of
your costs associated with expenses for renting and

maintaining the property from the total income you have. This provides you with a budget for shopping for a property to rent. Keep in mind that you may need to adjust these numbers somewhat later on, both up and down, as costs change and you get a more realistic view of the costs. You may not want to cut it too close.

How Much Can You Afford?

Deciding how much apartment they can afford is one of the most important decisions a renter will have to make. This decision will help to determine a number of factors include the size and location of the potential apartment as well as the types of amenities offered. Those who are interested in renting an apartment will have to consider all of their current expenses in comparison to their monthly cash flow. They will also have to determine whether or not there are changes they can make to their current budget to make a larger or more well situated apartment affordable.

Consider All of Your Expenses

When deciding how much apartment they can afford, renters should carefully consider all of their monthly expenses in relation to their monthly income. Expenses may include, but are not limited to, utilities such as gas, water and electric, telephone, cell phone, Internet services, cable television, car insurance, renter's insurance, gas for car, cost of commuting to work, groceries and other incidental charges. Subtracting these costs from the monthly income will give the renter a good idea of how much money they can afford to spend on rent each month. Renters might also consider subtracting an additional amount out of their monthly income to give them the opportunity to save some money each month.

Expenses to be considered should also include expenses for entertainment purposes such as dining in restaurants, going to movie theaters or cultural events. Even movie rentals should be considered in this category. Considering these expenses is necessary because otherwise the renter may not allot a portion of their budget for such purposes and may find themselves unable to participate in some previously enjoyed leisure activities.

Is There Room for Improvement?

When examining the monthly budget, renter should take the opportunity to determine whether or not there is room for improvement in their current financial situation. For example a renter may find they are able to minimize their monthly bills by obtaining their car insurance and renter's insurance from the same insurance carrier. The carrier may be willing to offer a discount to a customer who utilizes their services for more than one type of insurance. Likewise there may be the opportunity to minimize expenses by bundling services such as telephone, Internet and possibly even cable television.

Also, consider entertainment expenses as an opportunity for financial improvement. If a renter currently eats out in restaurants for dinner on both Friday and Saturday of every week, they could consider limiting these dining experiences to only one night a week or even only one night every other week. This can result in a significant cost savings which may enable the renter to afford a more expensive apartment.

Other areas where renters can sometimes cut expenses are on cell phone bills and cable television bills. Examine your cell phone bill carefully. If you are not using all of your minutes each month, it might be worthwhile to switch to a plan with fewer minutes. This would lower your monthly bill without causing you to make any sacrifices. One area where sacrificing might contribute to more monthly cash flow is with cable television. Renters who pay higher fees for premium channels can consider eliminating these channels. All of these small changes to monthly spending can contribute to the renter being able to afford a more expensive apartment which may be larger or in a better location than the apartment they would be able to afford without making changes.

Is There a Need for Improvement?

Although trimming superfluous expenses is always a good financial strategy, renters should determine if this is necessary in terms of their rental situation before making drastic changes. Once a renter has established the amount of money they can afford to spend in rent, they can start to look for available apartments in that price range. If the renter is happy with the choices available to them at this time, there may not be a need to make financial adjustments at this time. However, if the renter is not happy with the options available, financial changes and stricter budgeting are warranted.

Sharing The Rent With A Roommate

Sharing a rental property, whether it is an apartment or a house, can be either a dream come true or a living nightmare. There are many advantages to having a roommate; however, there are also disadvantages. When these disadvantages are severe they can result in an uncomfortable living environment in some situations and even a dangerous living environment in other situations. There are a couple of ways a renter can protect themselves when sharing their rental property with a roommate. This includes screening the potential roommate carefully and including the roommate on the rental agreement.

The Advantages and Disadvantages to Having a
Roommate

Having a roommate can certainly be advantageous
in some situations. The primary advantage is
financial. Renters who opt to have a roommate,
essentially cut their rent in half if they opt to have
one roommate or in thirds if they opt to have two
roommates. This is ideal for renters who would like
to have a larger apartment but would not be able to
afford such an apartment without the assistance of
a roommate.

Another advantage to having a roommate is the
opportunity to share household responsibilities
with the roommate. Of course this is only an
advantage when the roommate is willing to do his
share of the work on a regular basis. If this is not
the case, it may result in a huge disadvantage
which will be covered briefly in the section on
disadvantages.

One of the most significant disadvantages to
having a roommate is a lack of privacy. Those who
live alone do not ever have to worry about not
having time to themselves while they are in their
apartment. However, when a renter has a
roommate, there is no guarantee the renter will
ever have any time to himself while he is in the
apartment.

Another disadvantage to having a roommate is the
distribution of household responsibilities may not

always be even. Roommates should have a discussion regarding the household responsibilities such as cleaning the common areas but there is always the possibility that one roommate may not do his share of the work. When this happens it can create conflict and resentment among the roommates. This conflict can make the living situation quite uncomfortable.

Select a Compatible Roommate

When selecting a roommate, the renter should be careful to select a compatible roommate. In the previous section we discussed how conflicts can arise when one roommate does not do his share of the cleaning. However, incompatible cleaning styles are only a small portion of the compatibility issues roommates may face. One important issue is entertaining. If one roommate has visitors at the apartment often, it can cause problems if the other roommate is not comfortable with this.

Even the times in which the roommates normally sleep can cause problems. If one roommate goes to bed early and wakes up at 4:00 am, it can be problematic if the other roommate likes to stay up late and not wake up until 9:00 am. In this case the roommates may not only begin to get on each other's nerves but they may also begin to adversely affect the other's job or social life.

Include the Roommate on the Rental Agreement

Finally, renters should be sure to include their roommate or roommates on the rental agreement. This is very important because it helps to protect all of the roommates. Inclusion of all of the roommates prevents one roommate from being able to ask another to leave unjustly. This may occur when conflicts arise but inclusion on the rental agreement ensures each of the roommates has a right to live on the property. Placing each of the roommates' names on the rental agreement also prevents one roommate from not making their rent payments in a timely manner. It will also help to prevent one roommate from being held legally responsible for not paying the rent on time by the leasing agent.

Extra Requirements

Now that you have some idea of what types of properties you need in terms of size and location, and you know what your budget is, the next step is to determine the actual desires you have for the property. There is no limit here; except for your budget and what is available.

Most people may wish to hold off on looking at additions that could be beneficial to you simple because they are unsure of what the market actually offers. In either case, ask yourself a few more questions before making the decision to invest.

1. Do you need specific types of appliances, such as a gas or an electric oven/stove?
2. Are you looking for a property that features a large living space?
3. Do you need a backyard?
4. Are you looking for a property that is on a specific floor or has a specific view?
5. Do you want a property that has a specific layout?

Again, these are just the extras that would be nice to have. You can let your agent know about these if you would like to. But it is very important that you keep a realistic eye on what is actually available within your budget range first.

With all of this information in hand, you can start to look for a property that suits your needs and desires. Before you jump in, take the time to at least work out the details listed above. This will help you to find the right property, within your budget.

Consider The Amenities

The amenities on a rental property can often be the deciding factor for many renters. The available amenities may make a less affordable property seem more appealing. Conversely a property which is more expensive may be considered worthwhile if the amenities offered are considered valuable enough to compensate for the higher price. When making this decision, homeowners should consider their own personal preferences as well as their budgetary constraints to make an informed decision. Before making a decision to rent a property, the renter should carefully consider which amenities are necessary, which amenities are optional but highly desired and how much the renter is willing to pay for these amenities.

What Amenities Do You Really Need?

Although many of the amenities offered by rental properties are not exactly necessary to live, there are some amenities which some renters would not consider renting a property without. An exercise room is one such example. While this is certainly not necessary, many renters prefer having this option. Without an onsite exercise facility, many renters would have to consider joining a gym for their exercise needs. This will likely increase the monthly expenses significantly and, depending on the location, may also make it inconvenient for the renter to visit the gym. An onsite exercise is significantly more convenient than traveling to a gym in another location. For this reason many renters consider the added expense associated with an onsite exercise facility to be worthwhile.

Some renters may even consider only renting an apartment in a facility that has a pool. Although this is not a necessity some renters, especially in warm climates, might only consider living in a rental property where there is access to a pool especially if the majority of rental properties include this amenity.

What Amenities Do You Really Want?

In addition to the amenities a renter feels he needs, there are some amenities which may be desired as opposed to necessary. A movie theater may be an example of this type of amenity. Renters may not decide against a rental property which does not have this feature but may be more inclined to select a property that has this feature as opposed to one that does not as long as the price is comparable.

A meeting space may be another example of an amenity which may not be required but that many renters are willing to pay extra to have. Renters who entertain frequently may enjoy this type of amenity because it affords them extra space for entertaining. They may be able to easily invite eight or more people over for a dinner party if there is meeting space available but this might not be possible if the renter were confined to their apartment.

Are You Paying Too Much for Amenities?

While some amenities may be viewed as necessary and others may merely be viewed as worthwhile and still others may be viewed as superfluous, the most important decision renters will have to make is how much they are willing to pay for these amenities. Comparison shopping may be the best way to determine whether or not certain amenities are financially worthwhile.

Renters who are considering apartments of similar size in the same geographic region should consider the amenities offered as well as the price of the apartment. Apartments of similar size in the same area should be fairly close in price. However, an apartment which offers more advanced amenities might be significantly higher in price. Renters should list the available amenities and use this information in making cost comparisons. This information can be used to determine whether or not the renter is willing to pay a higher price for such amenities. Renters who conclude the additional cost is not warranted have determined that the prices of the amenities are not worthwhile to them and they are likely to choose the more affordable apartment which features fewer amenities.

Furnished Or Unfurnished?

Renters will often be faced with the decision of whether to opt for a furnished apartment or an unfurnished apartment. The majority of apartments available for rent are likely to be unfurnished apartments but there are some apartments which are available with furnishings. There are some situations in which it makes sense to choose a furnished apartment. Likewise there are situations in which a furnished apartment is not a good idea.

This article will discuss these situations in an effort to assist the reader in determining whether or not it is better to rent a furnished apartment or an unfurnished apartment.

What Does Furnished Mean?

A furnished apartment may mean different things to different people. Some renters may expect a furnished apartment to have each and every room completely furnished with every possible piece of furniture. Typical furnishings may include a bed, a dresser, nightstands, alarm clock with built in radio, a television, stereo equipment, DVD player, an entertainment center, couch, coffee table, end tables, kitchen table and kitchen chairs. It may also include dining room furniture such as a dining room table, chairs and a curial cabinet. Others may assume a furnished apartment includes only the necessary furnishings such as a bed, couch, kitchen table and chairs. This essentially eliminates all electrical equipment as well as furniture deemed to be decorative in nature such as a coffee table, end tables or nightstands.

When is a Furnished Apartment a Good Idea?

A furnished apartment is a good idea for recent college graduates who lived on campus in a dorm room prior to graduation. These students likely have very little furniture of their own. In this case, renting a furnished apartment may be more economical than purchasing enough furniture to live comfortably in the apartment.

The overall cost of a furnished apartment may be higher in the long run because the renter may pay more but those who are unable to pay a great deal of money upfront to furnish an apartment might not mind paying this additional amount. For these renters, they are not likely to notice the impact of a slightly higher monthly rent payment but they would definitely feel the impact of significant purchases such as a bed, couch or dining room set.

When is an Unfurnished Apartment a Good Idea?

There are certain situations in which an unfurnished apartment is a good idea. This includes a situation where the renter has already accumulated enough furniture to furnish the entire apartment. In this case, selecting a furnished apartment would not make sense because the renter would have to find a location to store either his own furniture or the furniture supplied by the apartment complex. The cost of storage can add up very quickly. Additionally, the renter probably pays a higher rent to stay in a furnished apartment.

An unfurnished apartment is also a good idea when the renter currently does not have any furniture but is looking forward to purchasing furniture and has already saved up enough money to make these purchases. In this situation the renter will likely select an unfurnished apartment and plan on shopping for furniture almost immediately after taking possession of the rental property.

Storing Extra Furniture

Renters who opt for a fully furnished apartment when they already have a sufficient amount of furniture have to determine what they will do with their furniture while they are staying in the rental apartment. The options are basically as follows:

* Sell or give away all currently owned furniture
* Store your own furniture
* Store the furniture which comes with the apartment

While each of the above options is certainly valid, the renter should seriously consider whether or not they want to pay additional storage fees just to rent a furnished apartment. Renters who plan to sell or donate their current furniture do not face this dilemma but those who plan to store one set of furniture should carefully consider the price of storage. They should also consult with the leasing agent to determine if there are any contract items which prohibit placing furniture owned by the apartment complex in an offsite storage facility. There may be provisions which allow for these items to be stored but require them to be stored onsite.

Helpful Tips When Evaluating Furniture

Renters who are viewing apartment complexes are often led to furnished models which have been tastefully decorated. Although the furnishings in these model apartments are usually very aesthetically appealing they also usually serve another purpose as well. This other purpose is to make the room appear larger than it is. There are decorator and furnishing techniques which can make a room in an apartment appear considerably larger than it really is. The size of the bed, the amount of furniture and the layout of the furniture are all items which should be carefully considered when viewing model apartments. This article will cover these three items and will provide useful information for renters who are trying to evaluate furnished apartments.

The Size of the Bed

Determining the size of the bed in a model apartment is important for the purposes of evaluating the apartment. If you are unsure of the size of the bed used in the model, ask the leasing agent for clarification. This is important because if the bed used in the model is a full size bed and your own bed is a king size bed, it will be difficult to make assumptions about the size of the bedroom. The differences in a full size bed and a queen size bed may not be as noticeable but renters should be aware a queen bed will result in less free space in the room. If the bed used in the model is not the same size as your own bed, take measurements to determine how well your own bed will fit in the room.

Is There Enough Furniture?

When viewing a furnished, model important it is important to note whether or not there is enough furniture in the room. For example there may be a kitchen table and only two chairs instead of four. This may make the room appear larger to those who are viewing the apartment but they are likely going to be disappointed when they move in.

Consider the furniture in other rooms as well. For example a bedroom which only has a bed and a nightstand will be decidedly less crowded than a bedroom which has a bed, two nightstands and a dresser. Your furniture may not be exactly the same size as the model furniture but there should be comparable items in each room.

Does the Layout Make Sense?

Renters should also carefully consider the layout of the furniture when visiting a furnished apartment. An apartment may feature all of the pieces of furniture the renter expects to see in the room but may position these pieces of furniture in a way that is not logical. Consider the family room as an example. There may be a couch, an entertainment center, a television set, a coffee table and two end tables but if these items are positioned strangely it can be deceiving. Most renters arrange their living room furniture in a manner which makes the area conducive to conversations as well as viewing of the television. If the television is positioned where it is not viewable from any of the seating options, the layout of the room is somewhat unnatural. It is not likely to be similar to the layout used by the renter and therefore does not offer an accurate representation of how the space will likely be used.

Decorating a Rental House

Those who opt to rent a house as opposed to an apartment may still be held to certain restrictions regarding the type of decorating which can be done on the property. These restrictions may be stricter or more lenient than those typically enforced when a renter is renting an apartment property. This will largely depend on the preferences of the homeowners. Homeowners who do not want to see major modifications done to the property may place strict restrictions while those who want to see the property improved may allow the renter a great deal of freedom in their decorating options.

How Much is Too Much?

This can be a difficult question to answer when used in reference to how much decorating is permissible in a rental house. Many renters opt for a situation where they are renting a house as opposed to an apartment strictly because they are looking for more freedom in their decorating options. However, the renter may find this desired freedom is not available to them.

Some homeowners may allow the renter to make minor decorating changes such as painting the walls, hanging up pictures or installing decorative shelving. However, more extensive decorating items such as new flooring, knocking down walls or putting in windows might not be considered acceptable by some homeowners while others may allow the renter to perform such actions. Still others may require this type of work to be done but may place restrictions which specify all improvement work shall be done by a qualified professional.

Check with the Homeowner

When considering doing some decorating in a rental house, the renter should first carefully review all of their contract documents. This is important because the contract may clearly prohibit certain items. In this case the renter would know for sure that they are not allowed to perform these actions. However, the renter should not count on the contract documents to spell out every possible scenario. Therefore if a renter is considering making modifications to the rental house they should consult the owner before performing any work. They should also ask the homeowner to provide a written statement expressing their approval of the work to be completed.

The homeowner is the renters' best resource of these types of questions because the homeowner has the best understanding of their intentions when they wrote the rental contract. They might have specified that no renter can alter the appearance of the apartment without the consent of the homeowner but they may have meant for this statement to only apply to certain situations. In these cases, seeking clarification and written approval can be very beneficial to the renter.

When in Doubt; Leave it Out

If renters are in doubt about whether or not to perform a specific decorating action and are unable to reach the homeowner for clarification, they should opt not to make the changes. This can save the renter a great deal of time and money in the long run by preventing them from incurring excess charges for repair of the apartment and wasting a great deal of time making an improvement which the homeowner may ask to have reversed in a short period of time. This is why renters should assume an action is prohibited unless they have concrete proof otherwise.

Decorating a Rental Apartment

Those who live in a rental apartment are usually quite limited in the amount of decorating they are able to do. This can have the impact of making a rental apartment not quite feel like a real home. In many cases the rental apartment is painted a bright white and residents often feel as though this color is somewhat impersonal but are not able to repaint the walls to a more appealing color. This is just one example of the decorating restrictions which may be placed on an individual renting an apartment. There may be other restrictions and reading the contract carefully will help the renter to determine what is allowed and what is not allowed.

Review the Contract Carefully

Renters who are living in an apartment should review their contract documents carefully before they begin decorating their apartment. This is important because there may be some common decorating items such as painting or installation of shelving which may not be allowed by the contract documents. Decorating in any manner which is strictly prohibited may result in harsh penalties. These penalties might involve the assessment of fees at the conclusion of the rental period or possibly even eviction.

Most standard decorating items such as hanging pictures are usually acceptable but some particularly strict policies may either prohibit this completely or place restrictions on the type of nails which may be used or the methods of patching the holes. Renters who have questions regarding whether or not specific decorating actions are permissible or prohibited should contact their leasing agent before taking action. This will help to ensure the renter is not penalized in the future for their actions.

Additionally, if the leasing agent tells the renter it is acceptable to perform an action prohibited by the rental agreement, the renter should always ask for a signed, written document stating the exception to the contract. This is helpful because the leasing agent may not remember making an exception to the rule or may not even still be working at the property when the renter's lease expires.

Consider Whether or Not Modifications are Reversible

When renters in an apartment living situation are making decorating decisions, one of the most important factors to consider is whether or not a modification to the apartment is reversible. In most cases, the action is likely to be permissible as long as it is easily reversible. However, the case of painting the apartment is a common exception to this rule. Although painting can easily be reversed, most apartment complexes due not allow residents to pain the apartment in which they reside. This is because although painting is often reversible, the process of returning the wall to the original color is not always easy.

Irreversible modifications such as removing walls or adding permanent fixtures to the apartment are typically not considered acceptable when decorating a rental apartment. Although even major modifications are typically not completely irreversible, most leasing agents would consider modifications which require the assistance of a general contract to be permanent in nature. Conversely, small modifications such as nail holes to hang pictures are considered reversible because they can easily be corrected. Again, if the renter is unsure of whether or not an action is permissible, they should seek clarification from the leasing agent.

Consider the Security Deposit

Most renters pay a security deposit before they take possession of the apartment. This security deposit is collected to protect against damages which may be caused by the renter during the course of the rental agreement. The leasing agent may expect to need to do some minor cleaning or a few small repairs after the renter vacates the premises. However, a deposit large enough to cover the cost of more significant repairs is often collected to provide the leasing agent with some protection in case the renter damages the apartment and leaves it in need of considerable repair.

Should You Rent A House Or An Apartment?

Deciding whether to rent an apartment or a house can be a very difficult decision for some renters. There are certain advantages and disadvantages to each option. The renter should carefully consider these points when making his decision. Whether or not an apartment rental or a home rental is ideal for a particular renter will largely depend on his personal preference as well as his current needs in a living situation. For some renting an apartment is perfect while others find a home rental meets their needs best. This article will examine the advantages and disadvantages of each situation to help readers make a more informed decision regarding the type of rental situation which may be beneficial to them.

The Advantages and Disadvantages of Renting a House

There are many advantages to renting a house as opposed to an apartment. One of the primary advantages is this situation affords renters who would normally be unable to afford to purchase a house the opportunity to live in a house for a much more affordable price. Another advantage to renting a house is it may offer the renter many more options. Apartments are usually pretty standard in terms of size, number of bedrooms and number of bathrooms. Renters who have specific needs such as five bathrooms and three bedrooms may have a difficult time finding an apartment with these specifications but may find rental homes which offer these options.

Location is often another advantage associated with renting a house. Apartments are usually situated in more commercial areas while houses available for rent can usually be found in more residential areas. Many renters favor this situation because it makes their rental property feel more secluded. Many house rentals also include a backyard which is desirable for renters with children or pets.

One of the major disadvantages to renting a house, is there may not be a great deal of certainty regarding the amount of time the renter will be allowed to rent the house. While a contract may protect the rights of the renter for a certain period of time, there are no guarantees the homeowner will extend the contract beyond the existing terms. This means as the contract is due to expire; the renter may be given notice that the house would not be available for rent in the future. Conversely, this situation is rare in apartments and most renters are confident there will be the opportunity to renew their lease each time it expires.

The Advantages and Disadvantages of Renting an Apartment

Perhaps one of the most significant advantages of renting an apartment is the amenities which are often available when renting an apartment in an apartment complex as opposed to renting a home or even renting an apartment in a private home. Amenities such as pools, hot tubs, exercise rooms, saunas, meeting rooms and theaters are just a few of the amenities often offered when renting an apartment.

Affordability is another advantage to renting an apartment. Rent for an apartment is usually significantly lower than rent for a house. Although the apartment may be significantly smaller than the house, many renters find they are only able to afford these options.

A lack of privacy may be one of the most significant disadvantages to renting an apartment. Apartments are usually situated fairly closely together and most apartments usually share a common wall with one of their neighbors. Renters may find their neighbors end up knowing a great deal more about them than they had intended simply because the living situation makes it difficult to keep one's life private.

Having to contend with noisy neighbors is another downfall to renting an apartment. As previously, mentioned apartments often share a common wall with a neighbor. As a result renters may run the risk of having noisy neighbors who listen to loud music or have boisterous friends visiting late at night.

Rent To Own

Some potential homeowners who are not able to purchase a home right away consider rent to own options instead. A rent to own option, often referred to as a lease, is essentially a rental contract for the rental of a property which includes the stipulation that the renter will be given the option of purchasing the property at the conclusion of the lease. This type of rental agreement may not be worthwhile for all renters but there are some who will find this type of agreement to suit their needs quite well. In particular renters with bad credit who might be unable to buy a home otherwise and renters who aren't quite sure they really want to buy a home. It can also be a worthwhile agreement for homeowners who are planning to sell their home buy may not want to sell it immediately.

When Your Credit is Bad

Potential homeowners with bad credit may find a rent to own situation may be just what they are looking for to help them purchase their dream home. There are a variety of financing options currently available and it is likely even homeowners with poor credit can find a financing option but it is not likely this option will be favorable. Homeowners with poor credit are often shackled with unfavorable loan terms such as higher interest rates, requirements to pay points and adjustable rate mortgages instead of fixed rate mortgages. In these situations, it might be worthwhile for the renter to repair his credit before attempting to purchase a home.

One of the best ways to repair credit is to maintain good credit in the present and into the future. Most blemishes on credit reports are erased after a certain period of time. Renters who have poor credit can work on repaying their current debts in a timely fashion and with time their credit score will improve. During this time participating in a rent to own program allows the renter additional time to repair his credit and may also allow the renter to accumulate financial resources which will enable him to purchase the home when the lease period is over.

When You Just Aren't Ready to Buy a Home

Some renters opt for a rent to own program when they aren't quite sure they really want to own a home. In these types of agreements, renters are given the option of purchasing the home at the end of the agreement period but they are not obligated to purchase this home. This allows the renter to see what it is like to own a home without having to commit to homeownership.

Renters who are renting a home may learn a great deal about homeownership during the rental period. This may include information about maintaining the landscaping of the property and dealing with conflicts with neighbors. It may also entail caring for and maintaining a significantly larger domicile than most apartment renters have to maintain. Some renters are not quite sure they are ready to handle all of these issues and may use a rent to own agreement as a trial period to determine whether or not homeownership suits them.

When the Homeowner Just Isn't Ready to Sell

Some homeowners offer a rent to own option when they plan to sell their home but do not want to do so immediately. Some homeowners may be hoping for property values to rise before they sell their home so they can either regain the amount they have invested in the house or profit from the purchase price of the home. These homeowners might choose to rent out their home during this time and offer the renter the option of purchasing the house after a set time period. This enables the seller to earn an income from rent while they are no longer living in the home. The rent they charge to the renter is often enough to cover the mortgage and yield a profit making it a financially wise decision for the seller.

2.

THE PROCESS OF SEARCHING FOR YOUR NEW HOME

Now that you have a good idea of what you are looking for, it is time to start the looking process.

Where should you look to find homes or apartments that meet your particular needs? Before you can make a decision about this process, you do need to take into consideration just a few more things.

One of the most important things you can do is to understand how property owners work. In some situations, such as large complexes, there are numerous apartments available for rent at any one time. This may mean that you can find several available units in the same building (be sure to ask if the unit they are showing you is the only one they have open!)

These larger complexes often advertise heavily. Keep in mind that the more property they have filled, and rented, the higher their returns are. Often, these companies use what is called a property management system. This company will manage the property owner's investment, keeping as many of the units filled as possible. So, where do these larger companies list the units they have available?

- Look for the apartment complex's website where they may provide you with a list of available units to browse through online.

- Check out the local ads for apartments. For example, many of these companies are part of a larger group or will buy advertising booklets with other units. You can often find these available through the local Chamber of Commerce or your city hall.

- They may take out larger ads online, too.

- Many work through advertising agencies, especially if the complex is part of a larger company. Several apartment complexes may be linked together, for example.

What about the smaller landlord? These properties may be just as valuable for the individual looking for a place to live too. They may be owners who are working as landlords or they may be properties owned by one person and managed by a property manager. These smaller organizations still need to advertise to get the word out that they have units available. They often do not have the high budget that other, larger companies, have, though.

They may advertise:

- In local newspapers (local and regional)

- They may have a website, but they likely use some forms of online advertising

- They may use word of mouth advertising, such as in churches, libraries and in other local publications

As you consider which property is the right one for you, keep an eye on both of these options. Landlords of smaller companies, and those property managers of larger companies are both well worth investigating. You may find more for less with one company than you would with another.

Online Search

Most people are happy to start doing some research online for the house or apartment they plan to purchase. This is an excellent place to start since it allows you not only to see what is available, but also to know what the price ranges are. You can learn what to expect for your investment in this way.

There are a number of websites you can use to help you to find properties that are available. It is always best to start out with the organization's website if possible. For example, if you are hoping to move into a specific condo complex, then use their website to learn about condos available for rent there. This is the simplest, most straightforward method of getting more information.

Then, there are third party websites you can use to track down more information on the units available in your area. These usually require the apartment or home owner to pay a fee to list their property online. They do not cost you anything to use, though. There is rarely a reason to pay a fee to look at an available house or apartment to rent!

Check out the following websites:

- **Apartment Guide:**
  http://www.apartmentguide.com/ Is a fantastic resource for those who are looking for a property to rent. It offers nationwide help for those looking for properties. One of the best features is its search criteria. You can specify just what you are looking for and it will find properties in the area you select that match what you are looking for.

- **Apartment.com:**
  http://www.apartments.com/ This website is very similar to Apartment Guide in its

structure. This does not mean that both websites will have the same properties for rent. This too is a countrywide tool to use for locating both apartments and homes for rent.

- **Rentals.com**: http://www.rentals.com/ Yet another website you can use to track down property for rent. Those looking for homes, condos and other properties aside from just traditional apartments will benefit the most from using this particular website to locate a property to invest in.

- **Move.com:** http://www.move.com/ As simple as the name sounds, it accurately depicts what you can expect at this website. This is another website ideal for those who are looking for a property other than an apartment, though apartments are also listed here.

These four websites will provide you with a good overview of what is available in your area. They are easy to use and they can answer most of the questions you have. Remember that the ads for each property are written by the advertiser, or the landlord/property manager for the location. Therefore, you still need to verify this information since it is not third party verified.

Local Area Listings

While using the web offers its advantages, it is not the only source for finding properties to invest in. In fact, you may find a number of great properties located throughout your area that are not listed online at all.

Remember, landlords of small complexes and single family homes do not have a lot of advertising budget to spend. Therefore, they are unlikely to advertise online, especially on websites where they have to pay for doing so.

The following are a few more ways to find properties available for sale in your local area:

- **Your local classified ads:** These are one of the best places to look since it allows you to read what is currently happening. For example, if an apartment manager has a property open up, he might have to wait a month to get it out through other advertising, but just days to get it into the classifieds.

- **Local online classified ads:** They work just like the other classifieds but they are online, which makes them even easier to use. Your newspaper may have the ads available to you. You do not have to pay for these advertisements!

- **Check in with the apartments you would like to live in** and ask about any units that are currently available. You can also ask the property manager to alert you of any changes over time, so that you constantly know when units are readily available.

- **If you are new to an area, use local churches and other nonprofit groups** to ask questions and get to know what is available. Often, they may know the good and the bad about a particular area. For example, you may be considering a local apartment complex with well priced units. Sounds good! That is, it sounds good until you find out that the area is a crime riddled location. Getting to know the neighborhood first is always a good idea.

As you can see, there are a multitude of locations to find that great piece of property to rent and call your own. As you consider all of your options, keep in mind the importance of using several of them. While you may find enough options right out the door by looking online, it is still quite important to get more information and more options. There may be a gem waiting for you in the ads you have not looked at.

Helpful Search Tools And Queries

While checking out ads is great, there are a few more things to take into consideration when searching for ads online. Once you look at an ad, there are several questions to ask yourself. The more descriptive the ad is, the more information it will be able to tell you. You do not want to waste your time looking at apartments that are not what you are looking for. Unfortunately, it is quite common for ads to leave out the important details.

Before scheduling an appointment to see the apartment, find out some additional information. You can do this by using any tools provided to you including:

- Any photos provided in the ads
- Any written descriptions provided in the ads
- Any videos found of the property online (this is common in more affluent complexes)
- And, by calling the apartment owner or rental manager and requesting the information that is missing.

Now, with the tools you have, there are several questions you need to ask:

1. Does this property fit the needs that I currently have in size and location?
2. Are any of the costs associated with the property, including rent, available? If so, do they fit within your estimated budget?
3. Carefully consider the property. Pictures can tell you much more than you think. Look at ceilings for water damage. Check the carpeting for stains. What is the layout like?
4. Is the unit readily able to be seen?
5. What are other properties in the area being rented at? You can compare other ads you see to this property. If it is lower, why? If it is higher in price, question why.

Learn to be a bit more investigative when looking at the properties that are on the market to rent. The more you can get out of the landlords or property rental companies the better, before you make the time to see the facility.

Issues On Landlord

As you consider all of the properties on the market to rent, you are likely to have to make a few calls to really learn how well the apartment or the home fits your needs. In doing so, there is one thing to keep in mind. How well does the property manager or landlord treat you? If they are rude, obnoxious or you feel like you are bothering them, chances are good they are not the right people to work with!

The way they treat you now is a good indication of how they will treat you later, when it counts!

As you look at the properties available in your area to rent, keep in mind that you also need to trust those who are showing you the property. As mentioned, some situations involve a landlord who will handle the showing of the property themselves. They could be owners.

In most situations where the complex is larger, you will work through a property manager. This person works for the owner of the property or with a property management firm contracted by the owner. In either of these cases, this is a person whose job it is to get the facilities rented. Therefore, it is always in your best interest to learn as much as you can about the location and those working there before deciding to move in.

One thing to look for is the company's history. You can learn more about the company by doing some basic research online or you can get more information from your local Better Business Bureau (which you can access online at www.BBB.org.) If there are complaints about a company or its employees, it is important to note if the problem has been resolved. This will give you the best indication of whether or not the company is trustworthy.

If you get the opportunity to see the facility, visit a few of your potential neighbors. Find out from them what the company is like.

What are you looking for specifically? There are several things to ask about or try to get a feeling for, even if it comes directly from the person showing you the property.

- What are the facility's rules and are they adhered to? For example, if there is a noise rule, but it is consistently broken, that could be an indication of a week management team.

- How well does the company handle problems or situations that arise. You want to know if they deal with problems, how and how soon they handle them. For example, if you end up with a furnace that is not working properly, do they handle this and if so, how long will you wait for them to do so?

- Does the facility offer on call help? If you get locked out of the complex, is there a way to get in? Is there someone on duty late at night for emergency problems?

- How strict is the company when it comes to decorating and painting?

- Does the property manager work regular hours so you can ask questions or get help when it is needed?

- Does the facility do background checks on those who will live at the location? You want to ensure that those who you are living with are people you want to be living with.

Besides knowing this about the company you plan to rent an apartment or home from, it is also important to know the financial stability of the company. Again, do some research on the company itself. If you have any questions, it is best to speak with the company directly and ask for more information. This can help you to feel secure about the company and living there.

Doing all of this research may seem overwhelming but in fact it will help you ensure you are renting a property that is top of the line in fitting your needs as well as a top company you can trust. After all, these people will have keys to your home and they will control a lot of what you can and cannot do.

3.
PROSPECTIVE
TENANT
APPLICATION

When you apply for a job, you take with you a resume. This detailed document provides all the information that a prospective employer needs to know to make a decision about you. You want the employer to see that you are a good fit for their company. The same is true when renting an apartment or home. You need to show the prospective landlord that you are a good fit for their particular needs.

Once you have checked out the property and you have done some homework on the landlord or property management company, it is now up to you to present a good case of why this company should work with you. It is not an easy process and yet, it is one of the most important things you can do for your rental needs.

In some areas, competition for top of the line and affordable properties is likely to be a big factor in your search. The fact is, most landlords will look at several applications for the unit to determine which prospective tenant is the right fit for them. This is rarely done instantly. For example, if you have scheduled an appointment to see the location, you want to be ready to make a decision on it within a few hours or up to a few days after seeing it. Some properties will not be available for that long!

Still, there is no reason to rush into renting a property. In fact, the first step is to ensure the property fits your needs. The second step is to ensure the company is worth working with. Then, and only then, it is up to you to present yourself in such a way as the rental property manager wants you to live at the facility.

To do this, you will need to present a case for why you are a good fit. There are several things to include here! In this chapter, we look at the various ways that you can make the property manager think, "What can I do to get this person to sign a lease?"

Application Requirements For A Background Check

When you do find a great property, be ready to provide all of the information required to fill out an application. When renting, most companies will require that you provide your personal information so they can do a thorough background check on you. They are looking to verify that you are someone who they would like to have live in their apartment or home.

Personal Information

Specifically, you will need to provide your personal identification information. This includes your legal name, current address and your Social Security Number. This information is then used by the company to accomplish several things:

1. The company needs to ensure you are who you say you are. It is imperative that they have an accurate identification on you so that if there are any problems, they can report them properly. An error in providing authentic information here could result in the cancelation of any contract you do sign, without getting your deposit back.

2. The company may perform a background check on you. Depending on your state's laws, the company may or may not have to tell you they are doing this before doing so. A background check checks out your criminal background. Some facilities are more lenient on the number and type of convictions you can have to live at their residence. Again, the laws on discrimination of criminal history are based on state laws.

3. The landlord may want to verify your old address. If you lived in another apartment,

for example, they may wish to verify any data they can through that company. The laws on what can be told about you are specific to your state as well. Some states allow a landlord to ask questions regarding the type of tenant you were and how well you paid.

Personal identification information is usually verified through more than one form of identification.

Past And Present Status

The rest of the application will center around details including your past and current circumstances:

- Where do you work? This information is likely to be verified later.

- Who will live in the apartment with you? Their information and identification may need to be verified as well, depending on the specifics of the location.

- Past employers and other references may be requested

Fill out the application thoroughly and neatly. You may ask to take the application home with you, but filling it out on the spot may be better especially if you are hoping to get an apartment or home that is in high demand. Remember that an application is just that: you are applying to rent the location. As such, you are agreeing to be considered for the property knowing that the company does not have to rent it to you. Once you sign a contract, then you can consider yourself to be secured.

Character References

References are an important part of getting any property, especially if this is your first property. Rental property managers will contact your references in most cases.

These are designed to allow the manager to get a good idea of what type of person you are. They are not interested in renting an apartment to someone who is unorganized, unprofessional, or has trouble staying employed. To the landlord, you are a risk they are taking on. They are financially dependent on keeping the apartment or house in good condition and on the tenant's making payments on time. Therefore, the more information they can gather about the type of person you are, the more secure they will feel about renting to you.

You should provide at least three references. Good people to use include:

- A family member outside of your immediate family (such as an aunt, uncle or cousin rather than a mother, father or sibling) since they are often a more reliable source.

- A past employer who will give you a favorable review.

- A long time friend, who is older; if you are just 21 and trying to rent an apartment, choose a family friend rather than your 20 year old buddy. This will look more respectable to the company.

Be sure that you alert your references ahead of time to ensure they are okay with allowing this information to be provided about them. You also may want to speak to them about what they may say. For example, you may want to tell your uncle that a property manager may be calling and that you would like him to tell the manager that you are a responsible person.

There is no telling what people will say about you, especially if they are caught off guard. Therefore, be sure you select those who you trust the most!

References may be called, or may not be called. In either case, you need to have them available to place on your application. Therefore, take their names, addresses and their phone numbers with you when filling out the application. Be prepared!

A Credit Report Check

One thing you may not realize is that a landlord or property manager is likely to request your Social Security Number so they can pull a credit report on you. Again, your state may have rules about this process. The company may have to ask your permission and retrieve your signature on a form agreeing to allow them to access your credit report.

This inquiry is not to give you credit nor does it allow the company to make any notations on your credit report. Rather, it is for the property manager to use to determine what your credit history is. Some companies will not use credit scores while others will. In both cases, ensure your credit is as high as possible.

Many larger property management companies do have credit score minimums in place. If your credit score or your credit history does not meet their specific goals, they may not be willing to rent to you. Most companies consider past credit performance to be an indication of future credit use. If you have a history of overspending or not making payments on time, this will lead the company to believe that you are likely to do so again.

Work On Your Credit Score

As long as four to six months prior to your search for an apartment, you should consider working on your credit score. It has become an integral part of the process of renting a home or an apartment in most areas. There are a few things you can do to give your credit score a boost to ensure it is as high as possible.

1. Pay down any debt you can. The lower amount of debt you have, the better this will look. At the same time, do not close off older accounts, even if you do not use them. These accounts establish a long term credit history for you which is invaluable.

2. Do not open any new lines of credit, unless you do not have any or many. You do not want to have your credit score drop because you are opening several new lines of credit close to each other. If you have very limited credit, you may wish to get a new line of credit, such as a credit card, to help establish your credit history. Use it one or two times a month and pay off the balance in full at the end of the month.

3. Make on time payments. The largest factor affecting credit scores is your ability to make payments on time. If you have been late in the past, establish more consistent payments going forward. This will provide

you with the strongest evidence of your overall ability to pay your landlord on time every month!

4. Check your credit report. You can do this by visiting each of the three national credit reporting agencies and requesting a free copy. To do that, visit FreeAnnualCreditReport.com, the only service associated with getting this free, no obligation credit reports for those in the United States. There, request a copy of each report, including one from TransUnion, Equifax and Experian. Look through the report for errors or information that is not correct. Then, contact the credit reporting agencies through their website to report any discrepancies. These are usually removed within 30 to 45 days and can give you a nice boost in terms of your credit score if they are significant information.

5. Use credit but do so wisely. Whenever possible, pay off your full balance each month. This shows that you are capable of using credit but that you do so within reasonable limits.

Note that your credit report is an integral part of your application for renting a home or an apartment. Therefore, do not skip this step of cleaning up your credit if possible. You want to put your best food forward especially if you hope to get into a highly competitive unit.

If you are unsure if you will qualify for an apartment based on your specific credit score, you may ask the property manager about their requirements. Outright ask if the company if they verify credit scores and use credit histories and what their minimal requirements are. This is an important step since you do not want to waste your time applying for a loan you may not qualify for.

Your Credit History

Note that even individual owner landlords do still do credit checks. Most of these companies will only use a credit history (not necessarily the score) to check out what is happening with you.

They are looking for:

- Your ability to make your committed monthly payments on time.
- The number and amount of debts you have to pay (do you really have enough money to pay these obligations plus the new rental payment?)
- How long you have had credit
- How much money you owe (If you owe a great deal, you may be on the verge of bankruptcy, which is likely to be a deal breaker for most companies.)

- They also use these reports to ensure that you are who you say you are.

All of this credit information is just one part of the application process. Some companies make it a more important part of the process than others do. As you consider the various methods to improving your credit and your chances to rent, remember that there are other factors that have to align properly as well before you can get into the property you are hoping to!

Income And Employer Information

Another part of your rental resume needs to be your income and employer information. Most rental applications will request this information from you since it allows the company to learn what qualifications you have for actually affordable the property you are renting. Consider it: would any business allow you to buy a place to live without you demonstrating your ability to pay the bills?

Your employment information is gathered on the rental application. You will need to provide information on your current employer, including the employer's name, manager's name, the address and contact information for your supervisor. This information helps the employer to contact the company and ask for additional information.

In some areas of the country, your employer will not be allowed to provide many details about your employment. They may be able to state your dates of employment and provide basic feedback on you. In other situations, they can verify income, your position and your work history but only if you have provide written approval for such a request. Of course, if a rental company asks for this information, it is best to provide it to ensure that you are able to qualify for the property.

It is important that the information that you provide with your application is accurate. There is no benefit to lying about how much you make here! Also, most rental managers will ask for several weeks or even up to two months of paycheck stubs to verify the income you are making. You should bring these with you when you are viewing properties and filling out an application. This may help to keep the property manger from having to speak with your employer, too.

What about income? How much do you need to have?

The amount of income you have will factor into the amount of rent payment you can make. Every property management company and landlord is looking for a different number. In short, they want to ensure you have enough income to make the payments you need to make (remember the budget listed in Chapter 1) and still have money left over to pay the rent.

They know that if you do not make enough money you will struggle to make the monthly payments for the property. They will not allow you to rent a property if they do not think you can afford to do so. While this may seem limiting, since you may have a good idea of what you can afford, it is still likely a qualification for moving in.

The amount of money you must make is dependent on various factors. Some property managers will request to see a budget outlining all of your other debts. They may simply want to know what other financial obligations you have. Again, there is no benefit in not being thorough and upfront about this information since it does have to be verified. They can see which loans and debts you have on your credit report, for example.

In addition, you may find that limitations on how much you can pay in rental income is a good thing. If this is your first time renting a house or an apartment, you may be somewhat unfamiliar with the costs associated with the process. This can be difficult for many people to predict. Therefore, see these limitations as a good thing.

Most property managers of larger companies will require that your house payment to income ratio be under 40 percent. It is best if it is under 30 percent, but that may be difficult in some areas. This would leave between 70 and 60 percent of your income to pay other bills other than your rent.

Present An Actual Budget Blueprint That Explains Your Ability To Pay

If you believe that you have enough income to pay your bills, but your property manager's ratio is too high, you may wish to work out an actual budget to show to the manager. For example, if you have very few other debts and would like to qualify for a property but you do not have a high income, show them a list of all of your debts. This budget demonstrates your ability to pay.

With all of this information in hand, you can provide your potential landlord with all of the information they need to make decisions about renting to you. You want to assure the property manage that you are a good credit risk and a good tenant. Doing so will help you to get the property you want to own!

4.
OCULAR
INSPECTIONS

Part of the process of locating an apartment or a
house to rent is visiting several locations. It is not a
good idea to simply agree to rent a property if it is
the first one you have seen. While you may love the
location, it is still a good idea to have a few other
properties to compare to it.

Checking out an apartment is rarely enough,
though. You should know how to spot potential
problems with the property and what factors make
it a good investment. In short, you need to know
how to look under the surface to make sure this is a
good place for you to live.

Once you find a few apartments or houses you are
interested in, the next step is to set up an
appointment to view them. Take your application
resume with you with all the details described. You
may also wish to bring a digital camera with you.
This allows you to take a few photos so that when
you come home, you will remember what you have
seen. Most landlords have no problem allowing
you to do this.

What To Look For

The first thing to do when you visit an apartment or a house you may potentially rent is to get a look at the area around you. Did it take you long to get here? Is it hard to find? What is the outside like (clean, safe, with ample parking?) Get a feeling for what the lobby and the overall cleanliness of the building is. All of this can be done before you actually walk into the apartment itself.

Once you do, there are several things to consider.

1. **Size and Layout**:
   Do you like the layout? Walk through the home to see how it feels. Imagine your furniture in the space. This information is a first step. After all, if the apartment does not meet your specific requirements in size and layout, then it may not work at all.

2. **Damage:**
   Take some time to notice any damage to the apartment or home. Water damage on the ceiling, walls or floorboards needs to be taken care of before you visit. Look inside cabinets for mold. Check the bathroom fixtures for any signs of dirt, broken fixtures or other areas of concern. Since you are likely to be walking around with the property manager, you can ask questions about what the problems are and if they will be repaired before you move in.

3. **History of Apartment or House**:
   Next, ask about the history of the apartment or house. You are specifically looking for information regarding the overall maintenance of the property. For example, did the owner's live in the house before renting it? Where there any major disasters affecting the property? This information can help you to feel more comfortable living there.

4. **Rules**:
   Virtually every apartment complex will have some rules that must be followed. This may include trash, mail, and noise rules. There may also be stipulations on pets, visitors, houseguests, and the number of children living in the apartment. Ask the property manager about any stipulations they have. Getting this out of the way right now will help ensure that there are no surprises later.

5. **Neighbors:**
   Neighbors are an important part in selecting the right place to live. If you are looking for a quiet neighborhood to live in, you may not be willing to live next door to a family with several small kids and pets. On the other hand, you may be hoping for such a family so that your children will have someone to play with. Keep an eye out on

who is moving in around while you are viewing the property. This will give you a good indication of what to expect in neighbors.

Concerns on Neighbors

One of the major disadvantages to renting an apartment is the potential for conflict with the neighbors. While some renters may foster incredible relationships with all of their neighbors and never once have a disagreement with a neighbor this is not a likely scenario. Most renters experience at least one instance of dissatisfaction with their neighbors. They may or may not confront the neighbor about this issue but it is likely to cause at least some tension in the living situation. In some cases avoiding the issue can cause the problem to worsen. In other situations, discussing the issue can make the situation worse.

Paper Thin Walls

Although most modern apartment buildings are built with a fair amount of insulation, there is still the real possibility of neighbors in an apartment building hearing music, television, conversation or other noises emanating from a neighbor's apartment on a regular basis. This is due to the close proximity of the apartments to each other as well as the common practice of having at least one shared wall among neighbors in an apartment complex. Renters should be aware of this and make an effort to avoid noises which will likely be heard through the walls during nights or early in the morning when others are likely to be sleeping.

Being Considerate of Others

Consideration for others is one of the key elements which can make apartment living more bearable and less prone to conflict. For example, while renters are free to listen to music in their own apartment, they should limit listening to music at a loud decibel to daylight hours when it is not likely that other residents are trying to sleep.

Residents in an apartment complex should also be conscientious when throwing parties. This is important because the renter is responsible for the actions of his guests. Therefore the renter should ensure his guests are not causing discomfort for residents of the apartment complex.

When Your Schedule is Unusual

Finally renters who have an unusual schedule may have a great deal of difficulty functioning in an apartment complex. This includes, but is not limited to, renters who work a night shift and sleep during the day. The unusual schedule kept by these renters makes them more prone to being disturbed by other renters who assume everyone residing in the complex sleeps at roughly the same time.

Unfortunately renters in this situation may have to make an effort to make their living situation bearable. While discussing the situation with the neighbors is certainly worthwhile, it is unrealistic to expect the neighbors to remain exceedingly quite during the daytime hours. Many residents do chores such as vacuuming during this time which can resonate in the apartment of another renter. However, asking the neighbor to do these types of activities in the evening is not feasible because the neighbor would likely be disturbing a number of other neighbors by doing so.

This is why the renter with the unusual schedule is often required to make changes to make the living situation workable. This may include purchasing and using earplugs while sleeping or investing in a white noise machine which can help to drowned out ambient noise and make the environment more conducive to sleeping. Additionally, the renter with the unusual schedule should make an effort to be quite during hours in which they are awake but the majority of neighbors are likely sleeping.

6. **Past Costs:**
   Ask the property manager to give you a run down on the costs associated with the upkeep of the property. Often, they have a good idea of what your average costs for electricity, gas, and other utilities will be. They can give you a good idea of what you can expect. This can help you to ensure these costs are in line with what you have budgeted for.

7. **What's Included:**
   Many apartment complexes come with included amenities or costs. Even in some basic apartments, the water, electricity, sewer, heat, gas, and other utilities may be paid for through your rental payment or may be a part of that cost. This affects your budget. Also ask about any additional facilities and amenities such as playgrounds for the kids, swimming pools, and even high end benefits such as concierge services.

8. **Issues On Maintenance:**
   Maintenance on a rental property can be a confusing issue. Renters may mistakenly assume all maintenance is the responsibility of the leasing agent and maintenance staff but this is usually not true. In many cases the leasing agent and maintenance staff are responsible for maintaining the common areas and performing major repairs on the apartments but the renters do typically have

some responsibilities. These responsibilities are often defined in the rental agreement and the renter should familiarize himself with this document to verify his rights if a dispute arises.

Renter Responsibilities

Typically renters have the responsibility of maintaining their apartment and the surrounding area. This may include the interior of the apartment as well as deck or patio space. However, maintenance of these areas applies to generally cleanliness only and not issues such as painting or repairs to the exterior or the interior of the apartment structure or the appliances within the apartment.

Additionally, renters are responsible for small repairs in their home. This may include plunging a clogged toilet or changing a light bulb. However, if there are any duties a renter feels uncomfortable performing such as changing a light bulb in a high location, the renter should contact the maintenance staff for assistance.

Renters also have a responsibility to show common courtesy to other renters by not intentionally damaging or otherwise marring public areas. This includes vandalism, littering and even failure to pick up after dogs. Renters who fail to follow these rules of common courtesy may be subject to fines or other penalties according to the rental agreement.

Leasing Agent Responsibilities

The leasing agent and maintenance staff are generally held responsible for major items such as repairs to the exterior of the building, fixing appliances which are malfunctioning and dealing with plumbing issues such as leaky pipes. Additionally, the maintenance staff is responsible for intervening if the renter is having trouble with public utilities. Problem such as no hot water or heat to the apartment should be addressed by the maintenance staff in conjunction with the public utilities entity.

The leasing agent and maintenance staff is also responsible for maintaining the common areas. This may include keeping grassy areas manicured and other common areas looking clean and attractive.

When the Leasing Agent is Not Taking Responsibility

As previously discussed, the leasing agent has certain responsibilities to perform tasks and address concerns and complaints by the renters. However, when the leasing agent is not fulfilling these responsibilities it could create a harmful living environment for the renter. For example hot water is required to adequately clean dishes. This is why there should always be hot water to the apartment. Additionally, in severely cold weather the inability to heat the apartment due to faulty utilities or windows which are not properly sealed can create a hazardous condition for the renter.

Both of the examples mentioned above are situations in which the renter may put in a hazardous condition by the leasing agent's negligence. In these situations the renter should contact the Department of Housing to determine the proper cause of action to take in this situation.

In some cases the renter may be informed the alleged transgression by the leasing agent is not actually his responsibility. However, in other situations the renter may be informed that the actions of the leasing agent are a serious violation of the rental agreement. In either case, the representative can provide information on how to proceed to achieve the desired results.

Walking around the apartment and house is an important step in finding a property that fits your needs. Take your time. Look out the windows. Get to know the neighborhood. The more questions you ask, the better you will feel when it comes to actually moving in.

Compare Options

As mentioned, you should not simply dive into the first property you see, even if you think it is the best option for you. You should have a few properties to compare and contrast against this one.

You should request information on the property that you do not have. Also, ask the rental manager if there are other units within the same (or other) buildings to look at. There may be a significant difference from one unit to the next. If they state that you are viewing an apartment that is simply set up and not the one you will officially rent, never sign or agree to anything until you have done a thorough walk through of the actual apartment first.

In addition, if you feel the need to do so, you can have pest and home inspections done of the premises. These would be paid for by you, not the property owner. They can help you to spot any type of problem that may be unseen such as pest problems, water damage and electric problems. This is rarely necessary in most situations.

The walk through is often best done with more than one person. That way both of you can point out any concerns!

Once you have found the property that is right for you, it is nearly time to sign on the dotted line.

5.
NEGOTIATING THE CONTRACT

Once you find an apartment or a home you wish to rent, the next step is filling out and agreeing to a contract. A contract is not something to just simply agree to and sign on the dotted line. It is an opportunity for you to work through any concerns you may have and a time for you to negotiate any terms that are not going to work.

Even larger property managers will use contracts that can be changed from one tenant to the next, to accommodate specific concerns. In most cases, you will not be able to use your own since it is the discretion of the landlord and property owner to state his or her stipulations on what terms the contract has. If you do not agree to them, they will not rent to you in some cases. That does not mean there is no room for movement!

Have all application details been submitted? Have you been approved for renting the apartment? If this has not happened yet, it is important for you to ensure that is done prior to signing the contract. It can protect you in some situations. For example, you may find that the contract adds on to the cost in the form of an insurance if your credit score falls below a set amount. You do not want to agree to this. Be sure you have been approved to live in the complex before you sign the contract.

Your Rights And The Rights Of The Owner

As mentioned, the property owner has the right to dictate which contract is used, but he or she can make changes to the terms of that contract. It is your right to read through the contract at length before agreeing to the stipulations within it. You also should have the right to walk away from the contract, assuming that you do not agree to the terms and they cannot be changed. Once you sign a contract, though, you are agreeing to follow the agreement's terms and a landlord can take you to court for not doing so.

Contract Terms To Scrutinize

You should expect the following to be found in a contract. Take a few minutes to consider the terms in each of these areas.

Deposit Requirements

Nearly all apartment complexes and most house rentals will require the use of a deposit. A Deposit is paid to the property manager and these funds are to be held in escrow (though some smaller companies may not actually do so.) The deposit is likely to be at least one month's rent. These funds do not count as rent though. Rather, the funds are used only when needed. The stipulations of the deposit's use should be included in the contract. They generally include:

- The deposit may be used to repair significant damage to the apartment caused by the tenant
- To pay rent on final rental payments if the client does not make payment
- To cover any damage incurred to the property after the tenant moves out. The final walk through inspection is noted here.

The deposit has to be used according to the terms of the contract, but be sure the wording clearly outlines how. Do not assume the company will have your best intentions here.

Payment Terms

The amount of rent paid each month must be listed
in the contract. It must specifically state the amount
to be paid, the date the funds are to be paid, how
the funds must be submitted to the company and
the late charges, if applicable on funds not sent by a
specific date. These details will help ensure the
company receives the rent they way they would
like to.

Generally, the payment terms will be fully
described in a significant portion of the contract. If
they are misleading or unclear, clarify them and
ensure they accurately documented in the contract
before you sign the contract.

Rental Fees

There may be upfront fees that you need to pay
prior to getting the rental agreement. For example,
many companies require that you pay a fee for
submitting an application. There may be a fee
associated with pulling your credit report. If you
are to sign an application or a contract, note any
other fees that may be listed. You should know all
of the details associated with the renting of this
property!

Termination Information

Every contract needs to have information on its termination. The contract should have a start and end date listed. This will likely be for six months or one year, though some contracts may be monthly while others are longer. Besides this, the contract needs to stipulate which other methods the contract may be terminated in.

- What right does the tenant have to terminate the contract? This may include instances when the property is no longer safe or the landlord failed to meet specific obligations.

- What right does the landlord have to terminate? Here, as the applicant, you need to be more careful about wording. You do not want the landlord to have the right to terminate at any time. Rather, they may be able to do so if you fail to pay the rent, because significant problems in the complex or you cause significant damage to the property.

Learn what these termination stipulations are before you agree to any contract terms. After all, you do not want the landlord to have the right to throw you out so that they can rent the property to someone else at a higher rate.

Moving Stipulations

Another area that should be mentioned in the contract is the stipulation of moving. This is not part of breaking the contract. Rather, if the end of the contract is approaching, you may need to give a specific length of time before you move.

For example, if your lease expires in December, but you plan to move in January rather than renewing the lease, you may need to notify the landlord that you plan to do so by the end of November. Some contracts do not include these details.

Breaking The Contract

There are times when you do have to break the contract. There are situations in which the landlord may want to break the contract to get the tenant out. There should be some rules listed as to what happens if this occurs.

For example, let's assume you need to move due to your job transferring you. Obviously, you cannot stay at the same location and continue to pay the rent. Since you signed a contract, the company may in fact hold you to doing just that. Legally, they have the right to do so. But, this is one area where you may want to negotiate with the landlord if you think there may be a time during your contract where you may need to move.

Be sure to ask the landlord to include a stipulation that states that the landlord will try to find another tenant for the apartment, using reasonable methods, to get the apartment or home rented should you move out. This may allow you to keep paying for the apartment just until the apartment is rented out. At that time, you will be able to stop paying for the rental.

Matters To Consider Prior To Breaking The Contract

Most rental agreements have a section regarding the renter breaking the lease agreement. While there is also likely a section or several sections regarding when the leasing agent can evict the renter, the section on breaking the lease should be of particular interest to those who might be in a position to have to break the lease some day. Renters should understand these contract terms so they can make an informed decision. Additionally the renter should consider all costs associated with breaking the lease. This includes both financial costs as well as emotional costs.

Understand the Contract Terms

Renters should review their rental agreement carefully before signing this document. The rental agreement is a legally binding document which should be given proper consideration before entering into the agreement. This is important because understanding these terms will be essential if the need to break the lease becomes a reality.

Rental agreements typically do allow the renter to break the lease but not without some form of penalty. This penalty usually comes in the form of requiring the renter to give a specified amount of notice before the contract is up and also requires the renter to pay a sum of money to break the rental agreement. A notice of 30 days and a lease break amount equal to one month's rent are common penalties associated with breaking a lease, however, individual leasing agents may impose penalties which are either harsher or less severe.

Consider the Costs of Breaking the Lease

As previously mentioned there is typically a fee associated with breaking a lease. This fee is often set equal to one month's rent. While paying this fee may seem excessive there are some instances in which it is an economically good decision to break the contract even though there is a financial penalty imposed.

Consider the example of a homeowner who is the process or relocating due to a job change. The homeowner may opt to rent an apartment in the new state while the house is put up for sale in the previous state. If the renter enters into a 12 month contract under the supposition that it will take this long to sell the old house and purchase a new house, he may be surprised if his other house sells quickly and he finds a home in his new state rather quickly. This may all occur within a matter of 2-3 months.

The renter has the option to stay in the apartment until the rental agreement nears expiration and then start looking for a home. However, this option runs the risk that the home he previously found will not likely be available. The renters other option is to place a bid on the new house and plan on breaking the lease if he is able to close on the new house. In this case, the renter would be saddled with both a rent and a mortgage for 9-10 months. This will likely be significantly more expensive than the price the renter would pay to break the lease.

Breaking the Lease is Not Always a Financial Decision

The decision to break a lease is not always completely a financial decision. There are sometimes emotional components which factor into the equation. For example a renter may have only 1-2 months remaining on his rental agreement when he is offered a dream job which will require him to relocate immediately. Although breaking the lease that late in the agreement is usually not financially wise, the renter may make this decision to avoid missing out on a dream job.

Getting Your Security Deposit Back

For many renters the subject of the security deposit is somewhat of a touchy subject. Most renters assume they should receive their security deposit back in its entirety as long as there is no significant damage done to the apartment. However, this is rarely true as there are number of factors which contribute to whether or not the security deposit or a portion of the deposit will be returned to the renter when they vacate the premises.

Did You Do Any Major Damage?

Certainly doing major damage to the apartment such as putting holes in the walls, breaking appliances or tearing up the flooring may warrant the security deposit being kept but even in these cases the leasing agent must justify these costs. In other words the leasing agent cannot use one damaged item to justify keeping the whole security deposit. Rather the leasing agent is obliged to determine a cost to repair the item. If this estimate is large enough to justify not returning the security deposit the renter should be informed of the estimated cost of repairing the apartment.

Is Your Apartment Clean Enough?

All apartments should be cleaned thoroughly before the tenant vacates the property. This should include extensive cleaning of all rooms of the apartment including the bedrooms, bathrooms and any common areas. A cleaning should also include cleaning of all of the blinds in the apartment. Blinds can be rather difficult to clean and many leasing agents charge approximately $10 per blind if they deem there is a need to clean these items. This can add up rather quickly if there are a number of windows in the apartment.

Many leasing agents also perform a number of standard cleaning functions when any resident vacates the property. This may include items such as cleaning out the refrigerator, shampooing the carpet or repainting the walls. When these items are required, there is typically a fee associated with each item. In many cases, adding up these required fees results in a number which is likely already approaching the sum of the security deposit. Additionally, leasing agents often only allow for one hour of cleaning services to prepare an apartment for the next residents. This is rarely enough time to complete the work and therefore renters wind up being charged an additional fee at an hourly rate.

Have You Read Your Contract Documents?

Renters who want to have the greatest chance of having a large portion of their security deposit refunded to them should be very familiar with their contract documents. This is important while living in the apartment as well as while getting ready to vacate the apartment. It is important to be familiar with the contract terms while living in the apartment because it can prevent the renter from making decorating choices which are explicitly prohibited by the rental agreement. These types of decisions can be costly in the long run because they may result in the renter being assessed for perceived damages by the leasing agent.

Renters should also carefully review the contract documents as they are preparing to vacate the property. This is important because it may help the renter to clean and make repairs to the apartment in accordance to guidelines set forth by the leasing agent. Doing this will make it much more likely the renter will not be assessed exorbitant fees at the conclusion of the rental agreement.

Read The Fine Print

Nearly all contracts have some type of fine print. It is necessary for you to thoroughly read those details to ensure you understand what you are signing.

- When will your deposit be used?
- What obligations does the landlord agree to provide?
- Can your deposit be used as your last month's rent?
- What are the requirements for turning in your keys?

There are many other elements that could be included in a contract. Some may not be what you want. Be thorough when reading through it to ensure you know what is included.

Read Your Contract Carefully

Many renters barely even skim their rental agreement before signing their name at the bottom. Most renters are primarily concerned with the monthly charges, one time only fees, required deposits and other financial matters. Once they verify this information is accurate according to their conversations with the leasing agent, they often sign the agreement with no questions asked. This is a mistake because a rental agreement is a legal contract which may have a host of important information which the renter should be aware of before signing the document.

Considering a Roommate?

Those who are considering the possibility of a roommate may mistakenly believe this is possible because they are living alone and have two bedrooms and two bedrooms. These uninformed renters may see an opportunity to share their rent with another. However, some rental agreements strictly prohibit renters from soliciting their own roommates and allowing an additional person to move into the apartment after the lease is already signed. Renters who violate this agreement may face harsh penalties. These penalties may even include eviction.

Renters who want to have the option of a roommate should ideally make this decision before the contract is signed. This will enable the homeowner to put provisions into the contract to allow for the renter to add an additional resident at any time. The leasing agent may still require final approval of your roommate but this approval process will likely be dependent on the results of a background check as well as a check of the potential roommate's finances.

Want to Adopt a Pet?

Renters who wish to adopt a pet in the near future should also familiarize themselves with the rental agreement. This is important because restrictions on the types, size and specific breed of pets apply not only when the renter moves in but throughout the terms of his rental agreement. This means a renter who has signed contractual documents stating they do not own any of the prohibited pets such as dogs or cats are not free to purchase or adopt additional pets during the course of the rental agreement. Therefore, renters who do not have pets but plan to adopt or purchase pets in the near future should read the contract documents as if they are already a pet owner and decide whether or not to sign based on the statements within the policy.

Plan on Having Visitors Regularly?

Even renters who have regular overnight guests should familiarize themselves with their rental agreement before signing the document. This is important because frequent guests may actually be considered residents in some situations. This will likely depend on the specific rental agreement but it is not entirely uncommon for leasing agents to specify that visitors who spend a specific number of nights on the property per month are considered to be residents of the apartment. This is important because the rental agreement may clearly identify how many people may reside in the apartment at any one time.

Visitors who are staying at the apartment too often may put the resident at risk of being accused of having additional persons living in the apartment. In some situations this might be considered cause for eviction. For this reason, the renter should be sure he is familiar with the terms of the agreement before allowing others to spend the night in the apartment on a regular basis.

Do You Need An Attorney?

Do you need an attorney to look through your rental agreement? In most cases, the answer to that is no. If this is your first rental agreement, or it is quite complex, it may be best to hire an attorney to just take a look at it for you. This is important if there are any areas you are not sure of. It is best to get your attorney involved now, to work out the details of the contract, rather than have to fight any type of problem later on.'

Most larger property management companies have fairly straightforward contracts. They train property managers to fully explain the contract to you. Again, there is never a time when you should leave questions unanswered, so if you have any doubts, it is best to hire an attorney to help you through the process.

Key Tip: Everything In Writing

It is quite important to ensure every detail that you discuss with the property manager is written into the contract. Everything should be in writing!

Just because they say they will agree to a lower rent payment or that you do not have to pay specific fees, do not trust that they will. It is one of the worst mistakes you can make, in fact.

Most contracts allow for details to be written in. Ensure they are and that they are signed and dated next to those written in portions.

You should have a copy of the contract that is signed by the property manager or the landlord. Keep it in a safe place to ensure you can refer back to it if there is a reason to do so at some point.

Bargaining Tips

Did you know that you can haggle with the landlord and try to get the costs down? Unlike going into a store and purchasing something off the shelf, you can polish up your negotiating skills and try and get the costs lowered. To help you to do this, consider the following tips.

1. Check out the competition. The best way to approach a landlord to ask for a reduced price is to show him that other units, of similar size and location, are going for less. Find out what other units are out there.

2. Have a good credit score. Being less of a risk is a great way to protect yourself from paying too much. Show the landlord you are a good risk with your stellar credit. Tell them you are no risk to them and therefore you deserve a discount.

3. Ask for a discount for paying all of your rent up front in a lump sum payment. You may save 10 percent or more by paying for 12 months rent upfront.

There are no guarantees that the property manager or landlord will be willing to reduce your costs, but in many cases, they will work with you. The more they know about you and the less risk they see you as, the better your chances are.

Remember, when it comes time to renew your contract, state the benefits that the landlord has in keeping you where you are. They do not have to renew!

Property Inspections

Earlier in this book, we mentioned the option you have for a formal inspection. That type of inspection is designed to check out the structure of the unit or home. There is a secondary inspection that you should consider: one with your property manager.

Most of the time, the property manager will want to walk around the property with you, to get a good look at what the property looks like before you get the keys. It is important that any problems associated with the property be written down into the contract, before you sign it.

For example, you do a walk through with the property manager and notice a hole in the wall. This is noted in the contract (and hopefully scheduled to be fixed.) If you did not do this, but instead just move in, the landlord may claim the hole is new, made by you, and therefore you are responsible for the repair.

Look for:

- Repairs needed in the ceiling, walls and flooring
- Cracked glass
- Broken fixtures in the kitchen, bathroom or otherwise
- Missing appliances
- Damage to any of the furniture supplied by the owner
- Missing clothing rungs or doors

Anything that is not there that would be assumed should be there, or anything that has excessive wear and tear (or is broken) should be noted in the contract. You can make it a stipulation that the owner replace or repair these items before you move in.

With your contract fully outlined and signed, you can start to move in! It is always important to consider the benefit of taking your time with the contract. It will pay off.

6.
RENTAL AGENCY SERVICES

Your area may have what is called a rental agency. These are people who work for you, or on your behalf, to find a property for you to move into. They are similar to a real estate agent in that their job is to help you to locate a place to live. In some cases, they can be very helpful to you, especially if you are living far away from the place you will be living.

What To Take Into Account

There are several things to keep in mind when using a rental agency to help you to locate a property:

1. Who pays them? If you are paying them, you need to know how much it will cost ahead of time. This is actually the better route to take. If a property management company is paying the agent, then it is likely they will try and encourage you to

choose a property within the company's units. That may not be best for you.

2. What services specifically do they offer? If you are paying the company, get a contract that outlines everything they will do for you (and anything they will not do as well.)

3. What experience does the agent have? Are they affiliated with any companies around the city? Ask them why you should specifically work with them over someone else or doing your own research.

4. Learn if the company does a history report on the properties. Do they do comparisons of local properties to ensure you are getting the best price?

5. Find out if they will negotiate the contract for you. This added service is nearly always a nice benefit.

Hiring a professional agent does not mean you can forget about doing any of the work it takes to find a place to live. The fact is, only you know what you like and it is always a good idea to see the property before you sign a contract for it. This is especially true if it is a high-end property, which agents are commonly used for.

CONCLUSION

Finding an apartment or a house to rent is a big step. It is often a very rewarding process, too. Give yourself between three and six months to work through this process. That is the best timeframe for being able to get your rental resume in check and for getting into a variety of properties to see them. Of course, this timeframe may not be possible in all situations. In all situations, it is critical that you give yourself enough time to compare all of your options.

Checklist:

1. Have you checked out your credit history to ensure that you look as good as possible? Remember, you could qualify for a discount if you do!

2. Have you found at least three references who will give you stellar reviews?

3. Have you worked out a budget that is affordable and fits your lifestyle?

4. Do you need to hire a rental agency? If so, check them out first.

5. Shop for properties, view them, compare them and only sign a contract when you know the property is the best one for you.

When you follow these tips, the apartment or house rental process will be successful.

Looking to get your hands
on more great books?

Come visit us on the web
and check out our giant
collection of books covering
all categories and topics. We
have something for
everyone!

http://www.kmspublishing.com

KMS Publishing.com

Made in the USA
Columbia, SC
19 November 2019

83498265R00059